I0218901

This book belongs to

Copyright © 2023 by Jenni Pearce.

All rights reserved. No part of this book may be used or reproduced in any form whatsoever without written permission except in the case of brief quotations in critical articles or reviews

Note for readers :

This book should be read at a steady, calm pace to ensure the listener is in a calm and relaxed state.

The adventure then unfolds to allow their mind to take on the positive principals of the story.

Text and illustrations by Jenni Pearce

ISBN - 978-1-7392833-0-8

www.thecouragetochoose.com
First Edition: February 2023

The Magical Boat

Jenni Pearce

I'd like to take you on a magical journey.

On this journey you can learn how to use your amazing mind to help you.

As you go on your adventure you will be adding new information, just like programming a computer or robot.

You might want to close you eyes or keep them open to look at the pictures, whichever feels most comfortable for you.

A good way to prepare for your adventure is to make sure that you are nice and relaxed. You can start this by taking in a long, slow breath.

Calmly breathing in through your nose, then slightly open your mouth and release all of the air from your body in a big, long, low, deep sigh, as though you are blowing a balloon and trying to make it go high into the sky.

As you breath gently you start to feel nice and relaxed. You can just let anything that you are thinking about disappear, and float away like a big balloon, just floating up and away.

As you watch it floating away can you see what colour it is ?

Is it your favourite colour ?

The balloon is floating away, floating away, high above the clouds.

Perhaps you can blow away some more balloons.

Now think about your hands, and gently wriggle your fingers making them feel all loose and floppy.

Just notice them for a moment and in your imagination slowly count to 3.

1   2   3

Make sure those fingers are all wriggled out and nice and relaxed.

Do they feel all floppy ? If not just wriggle them a bit more until they feel loose and floppy like squiggly spaghetti

Think about your legs and feel them go loose and floppy, letting go of any uncomfortable feelings

Relax and let go, imagine them like squiggly spaghetti

As you grow more relaxed it feels like you are floating on a big soft cloud.

Can you feel it like a big marshmallowy cloud all squishy underneath you.

It feels so soft and warm and comforting.

You now feel safe and relaxed and are ready to begin your adventure.

Using your imagination, just imagine that you are standing at the edge of a beach.

It is a lovely, warm summers day, there is a clear blue sky and not a cloud is in sight.

You can feel the gentle warmth of the sun on your head and shoulders, and hearing the sounds of the birds above makes you feel even more relaxed.

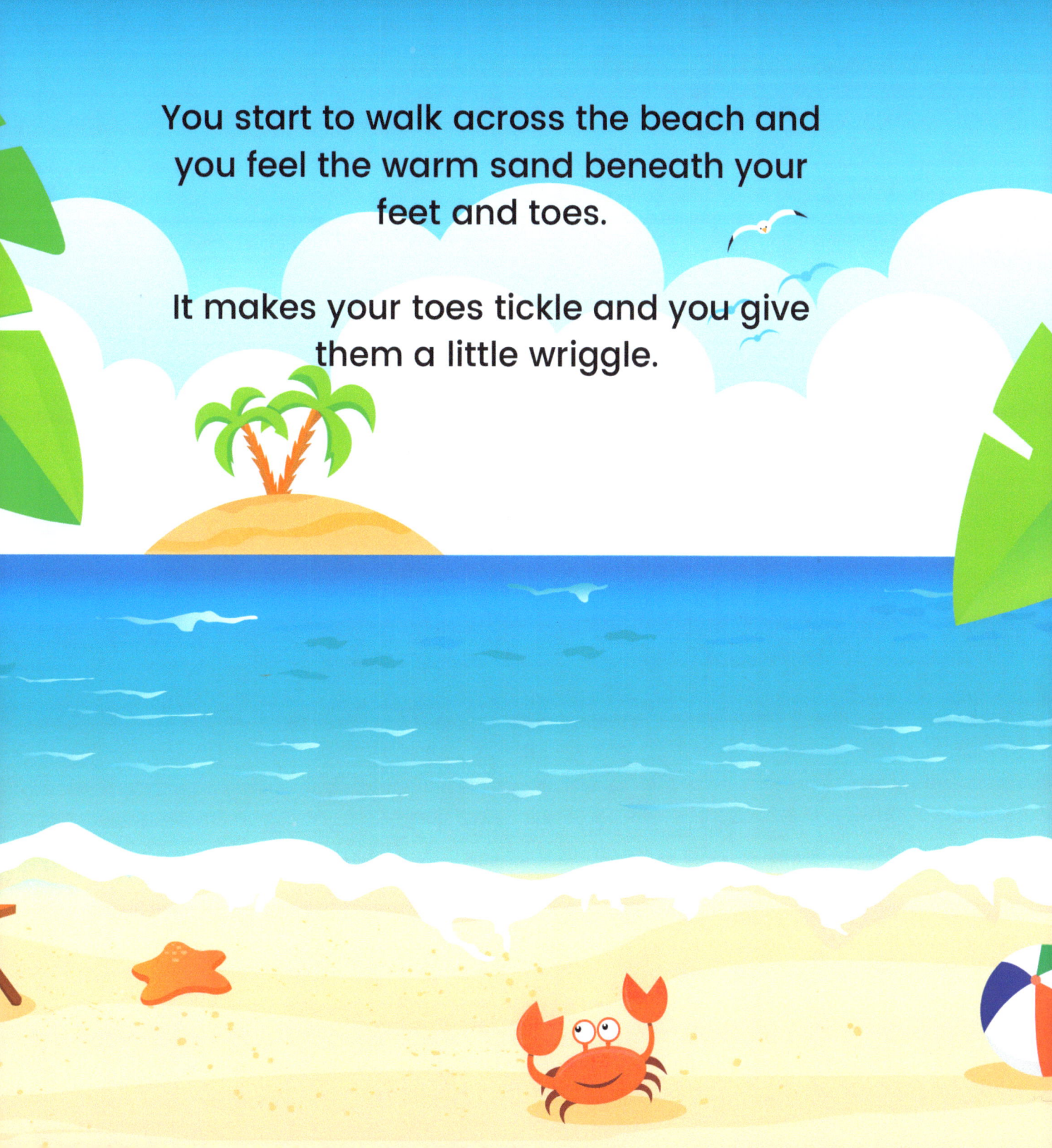

You start to walk across the beach and you feel the warm sand beneath your feet and toes.

It makes your toes tickle and you give them a little wriggle.

Stretching out in front of you is a beautiful calm sea.

The sunlight sparkles as you watch it darting off the tops of the waves.

It looks like the whole ocean is shimmering and sparkling with millions of tiny stars dancing and glittering on the water.

You continue walking towards the sea.

It feels so warm and comfortable in the sun.

As you walk you notice a sandcastle on the sand.

You walk past it towards the sea.

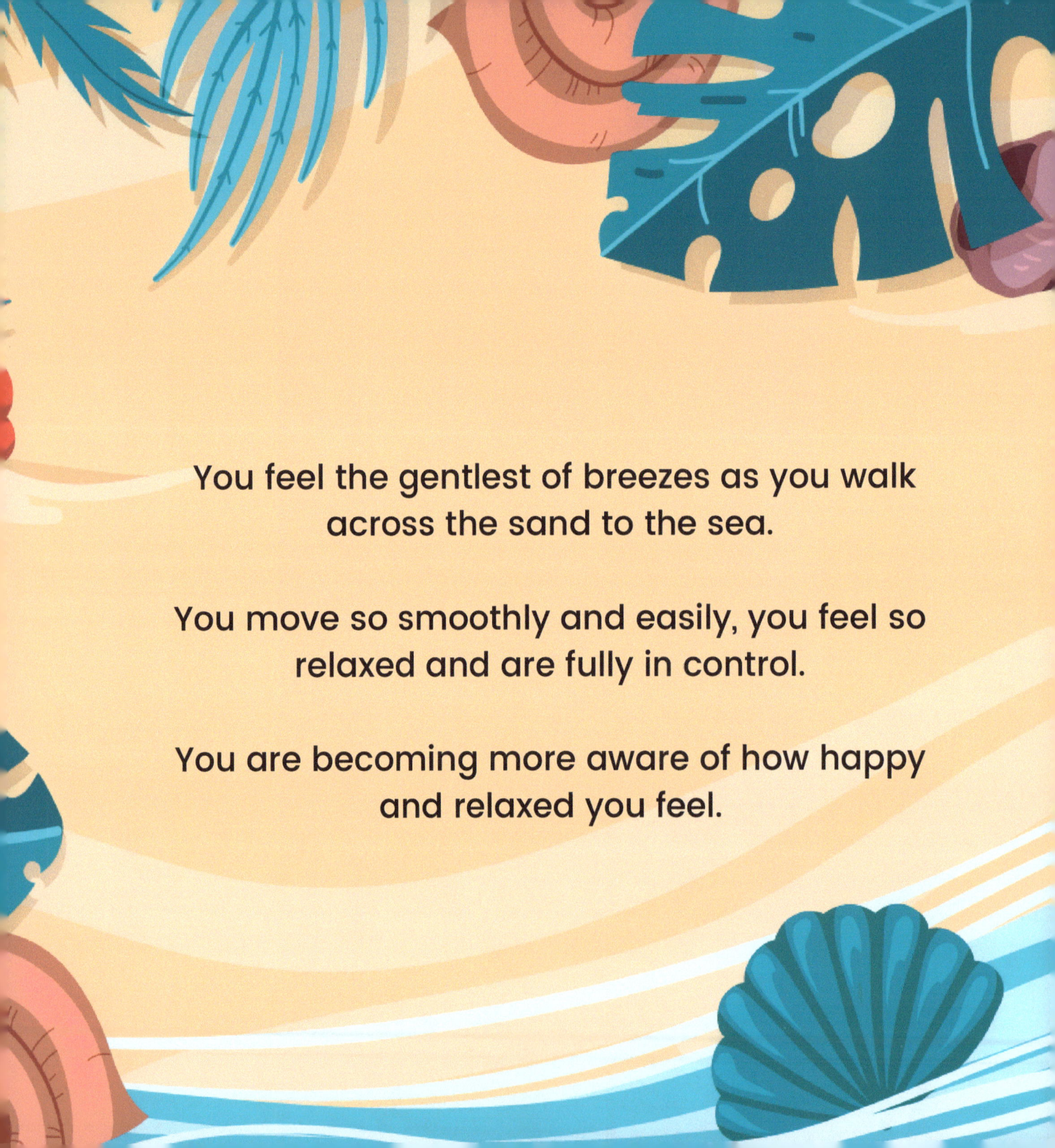

You feel the gentlest of breezes as you walk across the sand to the sea.

You move so smoothly and easily, you feel so relaxed and are fully in control.

You are becoming more aware of how happy and relaxed you feel.

You can hear the sound of the sea as you move nearer and nearer, and with each step you take you feel more relaxed.

You feel more calm, as you continue to follow a path that leads you towards the sea.

You look behind and see the trail of footprints that have been left in the sand behind you.

Every so often a bigger wave washes up and streams of warm foaming water wash around your feet, which feels so good.

You stand for a moment enjoying watching the water around your feet as you look out to sea.

As you look out to sea you can make out a small boat bobbing on the calm water. As you reach the waters edge you climb into the boat, feeling a wonderful sense of calm and relaxation.

In front of you, you can see the boats big wooden steering wheel and you take hold of the wheel knowing that you are now in control.

The boat moves calmly forwards as you begin your magical adventure.

You can feel the sun warming you as you travel gently forwards lightly passing across the beautiful calm blue sea.

As you look down into the water you can see the colourful fishes that are darting around.

The fishes look so busy with their busy lives but you are floating above them in your boat feeling very calm and relaxed.

Looking up to the sky above you, you can hear the birds soaring above, just going about their day.

You are able to see them but you know that you are going on your own adventure in your own magical boat.

As you sail onwards you see so many fantastic things.

Just let your imagination create them for you now and enjoy all the fantastic things you will see on your adventure.

Just take a moment now to enjoy this feeling and see what is there in the sea and sky around you.

You may see colourful fish or catch playful dolphins jumping around.

Just enjoy this special time just for you.

Remember this is your boat and you can take it wherever you want to go.

Imagine all of the amazing places that you could go in your boat, and all of the things that you could see.

Everything can just go on around you while you enjoy exploring.

After a while you decide to turn your boat back to the shore and start sailing back across the beautiful sparkling blue sea.

You see the sun reflecting on the water looking like stars dancing in the sunlight.

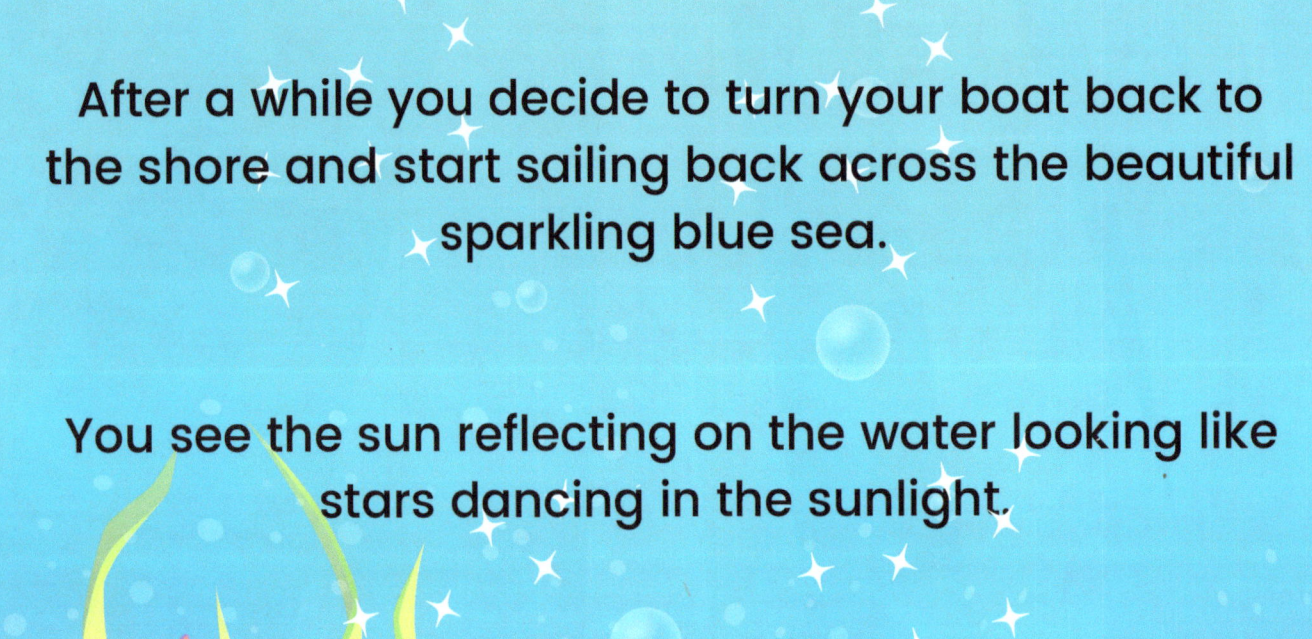

You can see the shore ahead of you as you sail towards it.

You feel so relaxed, yet full of energy, and before long you are back at the edge of the sand and you climb out of your boat.

You leave it safely anchored as you start to feel the warm sand again covering your feet and between your toes.

It feels so soft and so warm from the afternoon sun.

You know that its time to start heading back but you are safe knowing that you can come back to this peaceful place any time that you need to.

You are so excited to know that your boat will be safely waiting for you to go on another magical adventure any time that you want to.

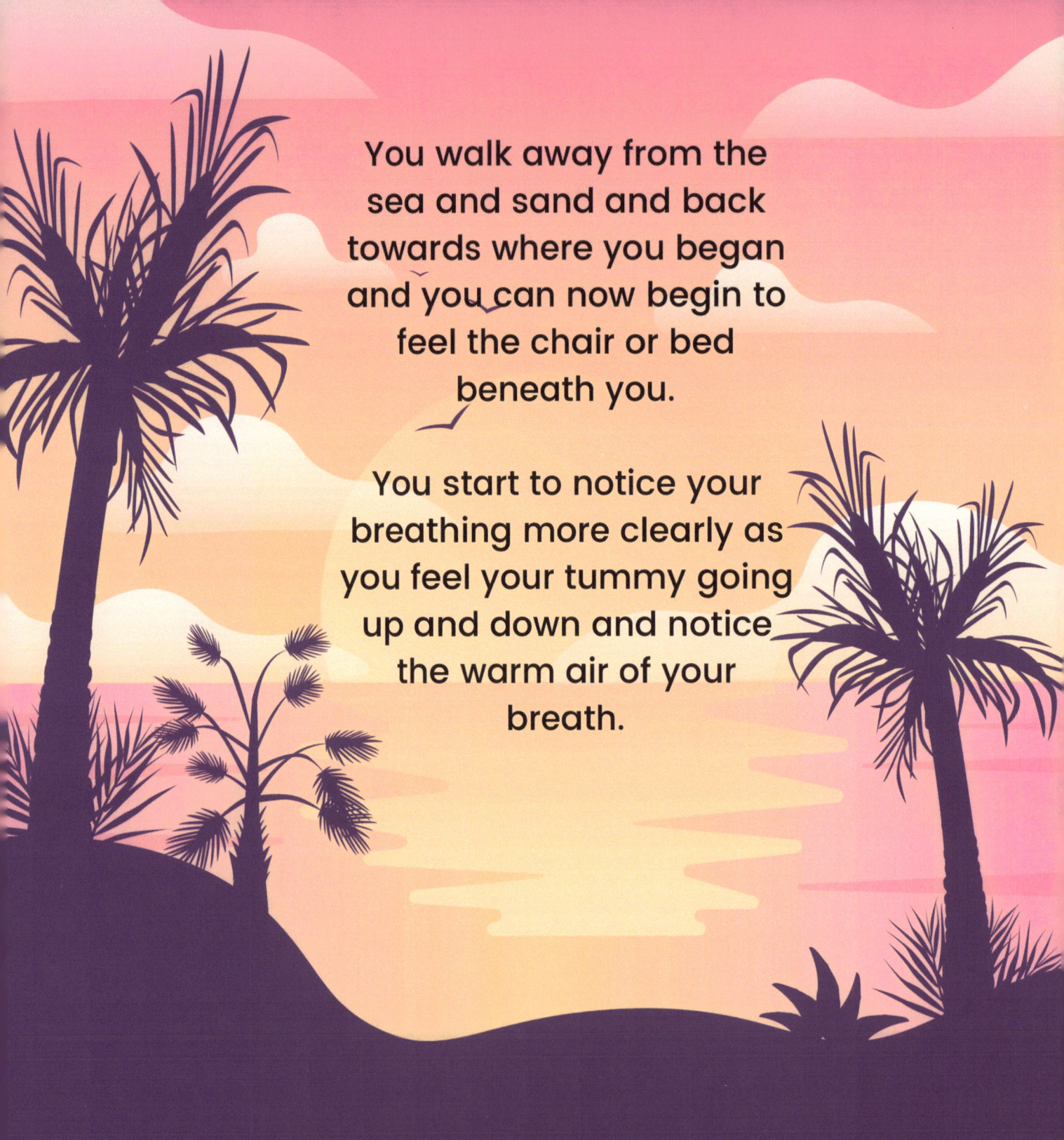

You walk away from the sea and sand and back towards where you began and you can now begin to feel the chair or bed beneath you.

You start to notice your breathing more clearly as you feel your tummy going up and down and notice the warm air of your breath.

You look around one last time and see the moon lighting up the sky, and you feel so calm

So soothed, and so relaxed.

Other books available in The Magical You series

www.ingramcontent.com/pod-product-compliance
Lightning Source LLC
Chambersburg PA
CBHW041245040426
42444CB00028B/103